STOP

DOING DUMB THINGS
WITH YOUR MONEY

To Collin,

Best Wishes & enjoy!

Cory

06/22/2016

STOP

DOING DUMB THINGS
WITH YOUR MONEY

*GETTING SMART WITH YOUR
INVESTMENTS IS EASIER THAN YOU THINK*

COREY HEIMENSEN, AIF®

The author has made every effort to ensure the accuracy of the information within this book was correct at time of publication. The author does not assume and hereby disclaims any liability to any party for any loss, damage, or disruption caused by errors or omissions, whether such errors or omissions result from accident, negligence, or any other cause. The information contained within this book is strictly for educational purposes. If you wish to apply ideas contained in this book, you are taking full responsibility for your actions.

Securities and advisory services offered through SII Investments, Inc.®, member FINRA/SIPC and a Registered Investment Advisor. SII and Olson Heimensen Financial are separate companies.

Neither SII Investments, nor its representatives, offer tax or legal advice. Please consult your tax and/or legal advisor in regards to your particular situation.

This book was written with technical assistance from Business Ghost, Inc.

Printed in the United States of America

ISBN Paperback: 978-0-692-67119-1
ISBN eBook: 978-0-692-67118-4

Library of Congress Control Number: 2016903773

Cover Design: Kendra Kunnari
Interior Design: Ghislain Viau

Note to the Reader

Dear Reader,

Money matters are gender neutral, but the English language (at least when it comes to pronouns) is not. Be you woman or man, parent, grandparent, child, or the Duke of Marlborough, this book is for you. And to keep that message clear (and to balance the scales), we will alternate between masculine and feminine pronouns throughout the book. "She" who saves money is "he" who saves money—and vice versa. Bottom line: *We all can save* when we stop doing dumb things with our money.

Enjoy!

Corey Heimensen

Table of Contents

Stop Doing Dumb Things with Your Money

Religion, politics, money. These three words hold a tremendous amount of power—the power to win elections and build nations, the power to demolish friendships and distance loved ones. Maybe that's why they've earned a reputation as "unmentionables" when it comes to polite conversation. Religion, politics, and money are the most personal aspects of our lives. They're so intrinsically part of our identity that they can be nonnegotiable, and thus difficult to discuss.

Call me unorthodox, but I think it's time to make a change. The fact is, we need to talk about these things—or at least one of them. And that is *money.*

The difficulty isn't just about social taboos. Most people just don't want to talk about money. Their reluctance comes not just from rules of etiquette but also from the discomfort associated with the subject. People think that money management—much like visiting the dentist—involves pain and sacrifice. They view contemplating investments and savings plans the same way they view a root canal: as a modern form of torture. And so they change the subject.

If you're like most people, you probably share this view of money. The more you put off talking about it, however, the more pain there is in the long run and the more you actually sacrifice. As long as you remain silent on the topic of money, financial security and opportunities fall by the wayside. That translates to money left on the table—money that could be in your bank account.

So let me ask you: What's going on with your money?

As a financial advisor, I see people doing many things with their money, not all of them good:

I see people making emotional decisions about how to invest. One aspect of emotional decision making is the grass-is-always-greener mentality that makes you believe that what your neighbor has is what you should have, and so you base your investments on their choices instead of on your own needs and end up losing money.

Another aspect of emotional decision making is being hasty during times of great need or emergency. It's challenging to think through all of your options during a difficult time, but often this is the time you need the most guidance and deliberation.

I see people withdrawing money from their retirement plans early. The main motivation of early withdrawal is to make ends meet. People find themselves in a tough scrape and need funds to get by, so they dig into their retirement savings—only to have that choice cost them down the road.

I see people putting all of their financial eggs in one basket. History cautions us to do otherwise (think of the dot-com bubble), and yet the practice of putting all financial eggs in one basket endures. People get excited when they see one company or industry performing exceptionally well and throw all of their money at it. As a result, they put themselves at risk for total devastation down the line.

Bottom line: I see good people doing dumb things with their money. Could you be one of them? If you are, what can you do to change your approach?

An Impossible Game

Like *money*, the word *investment* means different things to different people. To some, investments represent wealth, security, and the key to unlocking their financial dreams.

To others, investments represent risk, something they want to stay far away from. And to still others, investments are something out of reach, attainable someday, perhaps, but only once a certain level of wealth has been accumulated.

Adding to the confusion is the fact that finance and investing are not taught in school. That means that if you're like the majority of Americans, you look to family, friends, and the media for tips on how to handle your money. But unless you're a trained professional, the complexities of the market can be extremely difficult to comprehend. Your loved ones may have the best intentions, but what worked for them will not necessarily work for you. And the heightened rhetoric of the media often leads to even more impulsive decision making and more squandered opportunities. It can all seem so complex and confusing that it's no wonder there are so many dumb things being done with money!

But it doesn't have to be that way. In fact, getting smart with your investments is easier than you think. So I'm here to set the record straight.

Since 1999, I've served as a financial advisor to corporations and individuals alike. I've guided thousands of clients on their financial journeys. Through it all, I've noticed some patterns. Like religion and politics, these patterns might make for impolite conversation, but they must be addressed in order to make your money do the most for you. Isn't that what we all want, after all? Even if we can't agree on religion and politics, I'm certain we can agree that we all want to get the most bang for our buck and ensure a high quality of life now and into the future.

Time to Get Smart

You're working hard for your money, perhaps harder than ever before. And in an economy that's constantly evolving, it's important to find ways to help safeguard your finances. But with the myriad of misconceptions out there about how you should handle your money—and with whom you should entrust it—it's nearly impossible to get the returns you deserve.

I grew up in a small town with a population of less than a thousand, went to college, and got a degree in banking and finance. My first job out of college was in the accounting department of a large drugstore chain. As I gained more experience in the world of finance and investing, I realized that what I really loved to do was help people make smart choices with their money. So I got registered as a financial advisor and went to work. I started with one client and have now served thousands, all the while living in a small community in Iowa. You don't have to be in New York or Los Angeles to be a successful financial advisor; you just have to give good advice that works for people and helps them achieve their individual goals. It's as simple as that.

I've been in the business for a long time, and I've learned that most Americans don't actually know what they need to do in terms of financial planning and investing. And because they don't know—and don't want to talk about it—they end up making dumb choices. But you don't have to have a degree in finance to be smart with your money. Nor do you have to hand over the reins to someone else and blindly do whatever he says. It's possible to understand how to make your money work for you, and I'm here to teach you. Throughout this book, I'll show you how to stop doing dumb things with your money and get smart with your investments.

So let's begin!

2

Don't Buy More Financial Services than You Need

When you make the decision to see a financial advisor, you arrive with certain expectations. If you have some experience in investing, then maybe you expect your advisor to guide your choices. If you're just starting out, perhaps you expect your advisor to help you understand what you need to do in order to reach your goals.

Regardless of where you stand, at a bare minimum, you expect that your financial advisor has your best interests in mind. You expect that the recommendations he or she makes are based on what you need to do to make the most of your money. Otherwise, why would you see a financial advisor in the first place?

And yet most Americans receive less than what they deserve. Instead of getting personalized advice for their unique situation, they get what their friends, neighbors, and acquaintances received, what the stranger in line at the grocery store received, and what the next person in the advisor's waiting room will receive. Instead of getting a personalized plan, they get the same blanket services and advice.

And that, dear reader, is not OK.

Here's the dirty little secret that most financial advisors will not tell you: Not everyone needs a massive financial plan. In fact, a majority of Americans require far less than what financial planners will try to sell them.

Most advisors will tell you how to secure the golden egg of investments and make all kinds of money by purchasing the right product or service, when, in reality, the only person who benefits from these products and services is the advisor. The average person does not need all of the bells and whistles available on the market, nor does the average person need to pay for a full, comprehensive financial plan. Yet thousands of people are shelling out for services that do nothing but use up more of their hard-earned money.

To better understand this problem, consider the following: When you visit the doctor for an ailment, does the doctor hand you the same prescription as the last patient, and the patient before that? No way! If he did, he could kiss his practice good-bye. Instead, the doctor assesses your health and your symptoms, and decides what treatment plan will work best for you.

Well, folks, financial planning is a lot like visiting the doctor. People tend to associate the visit with pain and avoid it at all costs, but when they do go, they'd better be walking out with a personalized plan. However, in finance, that's not always the case.

Why not?

It all boils down to confusion. The market and investments can be intimidating and difficult to understand, but don't mistake that for inaccessibility. You don't have to become an expert in finance in order to know what's best for your money—and you don't have to do it on your own. In fact, you *shouldn't* do it on your own.

Finding *the One*

Now that you know you need a personalized investment plan, how do you determine who will deliver it? Finding the right advisor can seem nearly as elusive as finding the one romantic partner in the world. In fact, a good financial advisor possesses many of the same qualities as your ideal partner (minus the romantic intentions). Your advisor should have your best interests at heart, be communicative and understanding, and stick with you through thick and thin.

You can go about finding the right one for you by making a list of the things you want in your financial future. What's important to you? What are your goals? Your hopes and dreams? Your financial advisor should tailor a plan to accommodate the things you want in life.

Still having a difficult time conceptualizing what you deserve as a client? Consider my *Client Bill of Rights,* a list of the tried-and-true must-haves from any financial advisor you might be considering. The following services are what every advisor should offer.

You, the client, are entitled to:

- Ongoing monitoring and regular in-person reviews of your financial plans, accounts, investments, insurance policies, and applicable legal and tax documents

- Have your calls and e-mails returned within one business day (or sooner if the matter is time-sensitive)

- Receive accurate and timely statements of your account, including details related to every transaction

- Have complicated financial concepts explained in plain English

- Have any errors acknowledged and corrected without delay

- Receive only recommendations that have been thoroughly investigated in advance

- Be treated with the utmost respect and integrity at all times

- Honest advice and feedback, even if it's hard to hear

- More than just a business relationship—a genuine personal relationship that takes your circumstances, values, and goals into consideration at all times

- Have trust and confidence that your financial advisor is knowledgeable, registered, and up to speed with important developments that have the potential to impact you

- Be fully informed about all strategic decisions regarding your accounts before any change is made

- Have your privacy carefully guarded and your personal information shared *only* with those who are entitled to it.

Think of this list as the bare-minimum requirements for any advisor you consider. In fact, I encourage you to work only with someone who will agree to this list of client rights.

It's About People, Not Performance

When I meet with prospective clients, their first question is always the same: "What was your performance last year?"

"For which one of my clients?" I'll reply.

11

This answer is typically met with a puzzled look. Practically all advisors sell themselves on their performance. It's the first thing they advertise, their "shiny trophy," so to speak. What funny stuff am I up to, my prospects wonder, with this *which one* business? Their skepticism is understandable. But the fact is, every one of my clients has a different performance number. Why? Because every client is unique.

We tailor every portfolio and plan specifically to each client and his or her situation. Each one has a different mix of assets, timelines, and goals. There's simply no way to give a single performance number; I'd have to quote thousands of portfolio returns!

I pride myself on being able to help any person who walks through my door. I don't have an account minimum because I believe that everyone needs help when it comes to managing money. In fact, I would go so far as to say, the young couples with $1,000 to their name probably value their money far more than someone in a higher earning bracket. And they need just as much, if not more, assistance in growing it.

Everyone needs someone in his corner to show him what remedy will work best for his situation. Unfortunately, many advisors take advantage of that need, sometimes by charging exorbitant fees and sometimes by selling clients extraneous products and services. It's malpractice, and unfortunately, it is prevalent throughout society. Think about it: People overpay for all kinds of unnecessary services. They pay for the unlimited-data plan although they use their cell phone to watch only the occasional YouTube video. They pay for the yearly gym membership with access to facilities worldwide, and yet they go only a few times a month and certainly never when they're on vacation. They pay for the jumbo popcorn at the movie theater because it's only ten cents more, and then they don't eat it all.

The list of excessive products and services we pay for goes on and on. Money management is no different. However, when it comes to finances, people often overpay because they don't know what they need and they don't know what's available. You can get the products you need today without paying what your parents or grandparents did. Yet a lot of people are paying for things they will never use, simply because the community of advisors and insurance agents sell them like crazy. People just don't understand what they're getting.

It can be difficult to determine who can give you the plan that will best meet your needs, but now you understand why it's critically important that you partner with an advisor who focuses on *your* goals. Don't partner up with an advisor who talks only about performance, because market performance fluctuates. What's more important is that you have goals and that your advisor helps you meet them.

You know what you deserve as a client, and by the time you finish this book, you'll also have a comprehensive understanding of what you need in terms of financial planning. So the next time you see your advisor, you'll be equipped to go into the meeting with your needs and rights in mind. Stop paying for what they want to sell you and start spending smarter.

3

Don't Set Insane Goals

We're all familiar with insane goals. Most often, they come in the form of New Year's resolutions that involve figures with too many zeros and are set to be achieved sooner than realistically possible. Whether it's losing ten pounds in two weeks or setting aside $1 million for the old retirement fund, most people's expectations of what their retirement funds can do are wildly out of synch with what they actually can (or should) do.

Goals are good. Without them, we wouldn't have anything for which to strive. And perhaps the reason why New Year's resolutions tend to overreach is because we all want the best for ourselves. We all want to reach great heights. As blown-out as they may be, at the very least, these goals encourage us to make some kind of change. However, unlike insane New Year's resolutions, insane financial goals are a different animal—one that's far more threatening. Setting insane financial goals is an insidious practice that appears to set the bar high but can actually do extreme damage in the long run.

Like maintaining a healthy physique, having a strong financial outlook is a lifestyle that's built on sound habits. But as soon as you indulge in bad habits (in the form of insane goals), you're on a fast track to disaster that can require years to recover from. Knowing these traps—and how to avoid them—will allow you to turn what might be insane goals into achievable triumphs.

The Tunnel-Vision Goal

People view the stock market as if it were a casino: It's a get-rich-quick mechanism that works if you put all your chips on the right number. If you're lucky, you could go home with millions; if you're not—well, then there's no home to go back to.

Because of this misconception, people invest their money as if they were, indeed, gambling. Investments are not a gamble, not if you look at the data and statistics that prove long-term investing is the most pragmatic way to help safeguard your future. Long-term investing in good, sound companies are the best kind of security you can attain for yourself and for your family. But when you invest as if the market were a lottery, then you're taking a gamble—and you will most often lose.

I call this approach the tunnel-vision complex. It describes the person whose idea of a retirement fund is to invest in the hottest company on the market. People with tunnel vision are like desperate souls taking a long shot at the racetrack because they believe they have a sure thing. They get pulled in by the numbers, put all of their resources in one stock, and learn a hard lesson in the end.

Take the Internet bubble, for example. Investors couldn't buy in fast enough! And who wouldn't want to with such returns? Two of my clients, a married couple, had purchased an Internet-related investment that just kept growing and growing. Every month, they were adding money to their investment. Although these were very exciting numbers, they were making themselves incredibly vulnerable because a majority of their estate was now tied up in this investment. Despite my imploring them to diversify, they were so enticed by their success that they couldn't think of anything else. It was like an addiction.

Finally, something happened that signified the end of days. I didn't know it at the time, but I should have guessed the party was about to end when they announced that they had just purchased a new horse and named her in my honor:

"Miss Corey." When someone names a mare after you, that's when you know you're having too much fun and it's time to pack up and go home. And essentially, that's what happened to them—but not on their own terms.

Not long after Miss Corey had settled into her new home, their investment started to lose value. In 2001, it showed a 50 percent decrease; it did the same in 2002 and 2003. Their investment had basically imploded. From start to finish, they ended up with about thirty cents on the dollar.

The moral of this story is clear: Don't assume that your money is going to double every year (and don't name your horse after your financial advisor). These clients thought they had hit the ultimate jackpot and so they put all of their eggs in one basket. And where are they today? More important, where is Miss Corey? Out to pasture in some place far away, the last I heard. The owners exited the stock market, packed up, and moved to the country.

A certain percentage of people enjoy the speculating aspect of the stock market. In the grand scheme of things, speculating a few dollars isn't crazy—as long as it's understood that trying to go it alone and failing to diversify is just plain madness. The goal of a good advisor isn't to double your money; it's to meet your goals. So tell your advisor what your goals are, and you can put a plan together. Bottom line: If you set an insane goal of quadrupling your money in two years by playing the stock market, the advisor should tell you you're crazy.

The Bury-It-and-Grow Goal

The cautionary tale of Miss Corey's owners shows us that tunnel-vision investing will leave you vulnerable to loss. But there's another side to this story: what happened after they took their money out of the market. Because they played the stock market as if it was a casino and gambled their money away, they thought the safe bet was to leave the market altogether.

This behavior reflects that of so many people out there today, who believe that less is more. They believe that keeping money in the bank is a safer bet because the funds are always going to be there. Instead of investing, they choose to deposit their money into a savings account. They enjoy the security of knowing that their money will remain in the same place, earning the same (albeit minimal) interest, and be conveniently at their reach whenever they need it.

Perhaps you take solace in that approach as well. And to that I have to say the following: True, the money will always be there, but the risk is that it's not growing fast enough to buy you the things you'll need when it's time to use it. Indeed, when it comes to deciding where to keep your money, the following paradox holds true: Not investing in the market at all can be as risky as investing too much. By keeping money in the bank, you're not at risk of losing your money, but you are at risk of losing your purchasing power.

Long-term investing in diverse, solid accounts is one of the best ways to help insure your future because it's the only way to keep pace with inflation. When interest rates are as low as they are now, you need to invest at least a portion of your assets; otherwise, you're cutting yourself short by doing the equivalent of burying your money in the backyard—and then expecting it to grow.

The What-Worked-for-Them Goal

We pick up the majority of our habits from our family. They're the ones who teach us how to feed and dress ourselves; how to read and write; and, finally, how to be an independent adult. Many of these skills are reinforced in school—with the exception of one: financial planning. Your Home Economics course may have taught you how to sign a check or set up a savings account, but unless you studied finance in college, the subject of money was largely neglected.

That's why your parents play the most important role: because, for better or worse, your money habits are largely based on your parents' money habits. If they were good at saving and living within their means, then that could be a very good thing for you. However, the juncture at which this practice becomes insane is when you think that the means and mechanisms of their retirement will be the same for yours. Just because your parents knew how to spend and save correctly, that doesn't mean that kind of planning will work for your retirement.

The economy is always changing, as is the value of the dollar and how much money you'll need to live. Many of the services that are in place today for retired citizens most likely will not be there when it's time for you to retire. For instance, people who never saved any money have programs such as Social Security to support them. But you can't bank on that for yourself.

The greatest danger in assuming what worked for your parents will work for you is that it precludes you from seeking out the financial guidance you need. The discrepancy between the haves and have-nots in America comes down to education. The top 1 percent of the country in terms of wealth most often consists of the people who know how to invest and who are better educated about finances.

When your parents were putting together their retirement plan, there wasn't a whole lot of information about investing. That has all changed now. Since the dawn of the Internet, we have access to more information than ever, and that makes us feel more self-reliant. We decide we don't need to go to an expert because we can just Google it. We don't need to go to the doctor because we can look it up on WebMD. But with finance, that's just not the case, because even when the information is there, it's incredibly complex and difficult to understand. Google can give you information, but it's not going to help you get into a higher tax bracket. Often an advisor is needed to help make sense of all the information.

Many people understand the importance and benefit of investing their money in the market. What many do not understand is how to make the most of those investment dollars. Investing isn't a craps game. To do it right, you invest in things you understand—or that your advisor understands. And you set realistic, reasonable goals.

I once had a forty-year-old client come into my office to say he wanted to have a million dollars when he retired. So I asked, "How are you going to do that?"

"Well, I can save $200 a month," he replied.

So certain was he that this was the equation for a comfortable retirement that he had avoided seeking financial advice up until that point. But something was missing from this equation: the analysis. So I took him through the math and stretched those savings out into the future and calculated in such factors as inflation. As it turns out, that $1 million is nowhere near what he actually needs. He had to seriously reevaluate his savings plan, which was a huge wake-up call. Luckily, we made the changes necessary to set him on the right path.

The first step was educating him on his finances and dispelling some of the myths that had prevented him from capitalizing on his earnings. It's possible for everyone to make smart decisions with money. Even if you find yourself identifying with some of these insane goal-setting strategies, it's never too late to make a change. The key is to start early—and what better time than the present? Invest in yourself now to help secure your dreams down the line.

4

Don't Hire an Advisor Who's Not an Advisor

There are those who talk the talk and walk the walk. And then there are those who just talk.

In any given industry, you'll find professionals, people who deliver on what they advertise, and others who seemingly take your money and run. You would think that qualifications such as accreditation, degrees, and certificates would separate the con artist from the real deal, but unfortunately, that's not always the case. And so it's up to the consumer to tell the difference between true financial advisors and those who are merely imitating one.

It's up to you, the consumer, to determine who will give you the most value for your money. So how can you spot the true advisors? How can you separate the talkers from the doers, the professionals from the imitators? How can you identify an advisor who will not only create a plan for your finances, but carry it out as well, continuing to make decisions in your best interest for the duration of that plan? How can you protect yourself from those who pitch enticing offers but then essentially disappear after the initial meet and greet?

In my experience, imitators can be categorized into three groups:

- Salesperson

- Interior decorator

- Marketer extraordinaire

As seems clear, none of these designations ensure that advisors will do what's best with your money. In fact, they're not truly financial advisors at all. They just talk the talk in the first meeting, and then operate as a completely different kind of consultant going forward.

Warning: Imitators who operate under the guise of financial advisors look startlingly similar to the real deal. In fact, to the untrained eye, they can be nearly indistinguishable. To help you protect yourself and to increase your chances of connecting with the right advisor, I offer you a guide to weeding out the talkers from the doers, a guide to distinguishing the imitators from the professionals who can truly help you.

The Salesperson

Good advisors are able to answer any relevant question that's thrown their way. Their answers are in plain terms that their clients can understand. There is no ambiguity between what they're doing for the client and what the client understands they are doing for their finances.

The only way to achieve this mutual understanding is for advisors to be in tune with their clients' needs. Ergo, good advisors spend more time listening to their clients than they do talking to them.

Good salespeople, however, talk more than they listen. Salespeople must talk more because it's in their best interest to close the deal and move on to the next prospect. It's not so important that each client understands the financial services offered, and certainly not the details therein, because salespeople operate on their ability to win with words. They survive on their talent for boasting about everything they can do for the client and creating an air of confidence and grandeur. Never mind how the clients feel about their finances thereafter.

The risk of having a salesperson as an advisor is that the core, essential element—trust—is left by the wayside. How can you build trust with someone when you can't have a two-way dialogue? Salespeople may make you excited about their business offerings, but rarely do they take time to ensure all of your questions are answered and all of your needs are met—either at the first meeting or beyond. Beware advisors who talk more than they listen. Align yourself instead with people who not only say what they'll do, but also actually do it—with prudence and care.

The Interior Decorator

In any kind of transaction, we all want one, basic thing: to get the value we deserve for our hard-earned money. In our society, looks often carry the highest currency in terms of value. Something that looks good is estimated to be better for you—never mind the substance. America's "Fast-Food Nation" moniker is a perfect example. Junk food often looks and smells better than broccoli and carrot sticks, but really, it only sabotages our health. And yet our fast-food addiction is stronger than ever.

I call this *The Dilemma of Perceived Value:* That which looks good is rarely good for you. This adage applies to financial advisors just as well as it does to junk food. For example, some financial advisors place the utmost importance on having a luxurious office space. They will welcome you into their fancy quarters, filled with granite and marble and high-end decor, and wow you with their perceived value.

But looks can be deceiving. A financial advisor, after all, should be focused on serving his clients. Are the advisors with offices decked out to the nines really doing their utmost to build their clients' financial portfolios? Or are they more concerned with their design portfolio? This may sound bold, but I would argue that the fancier the office, the more time it will probably take the advisor to return your call. My methodology is based on the fact that when you define yourself by material objects, you're sending a message: You value surface over substance. As a client, you certainly don't want anything to do with advisors who operate in a pigpen (which is a different problem altogether), or with those who spend more time selecting the Swarovski crystal paperweight for their desk than they do with their clients' affairs.

People such as these might be great as interior decorators, but when it comes to financial advice, look elsewhere. You want true, absolute, definable value for what you're paying in fees, and that comes back to conversations and goal setting—the importance of providing information and dialogue over coordinating the parquet floor with the flocked drapes.

The Marketer Extraordinaire

Trying to decide where to go for dinner? Check Yelp. Looking for a vacation resort? Consult TripAdvisor. But when you are in the market for a new financial advisor, where do you go?

29

Many people assume that when it comes to selecting a financial advisor, all you have to go on is word of mouth or a leap of faith. This is a misconception. There are ways to gauge the track record of a prospective advisor, and it's important that you do so. Otherwise, you might find yourself consulting with someone who has a history of making poor decisions. This kind of thing happens all over the country in the financial-planning industry.

When a broker is terminated from his broker-dealer, there is often nothing to stop him from promptly setting up shop again, this time with a new broker-dealer. Or when someone fails in one line of work, she may decide she can make a go of it as a financial advisor. Crazy as it may seem, such people can succeed. That's because these imitators are excellent at marketing themselves. They're skilled at pitching themselves and projecting a confident image, the kind they know clients want to see.

Bottom line: You don't want a good marketing person; you want an advisor.

Of course, just because people are good at selling their business doesn't mean they're not skilled professionals. But unless you do some research, you'll never be able to tell whether this marketer extraordinaire is actually up to snuff. Public records disclose the very information—such as terminations and bankruptcies—that could influence your decision to hire an advisor. So always consult the records before you consult with an advisor. Good advisors do not harbor any secrets. They should be willing to disclose their regulatory history by directing clients and/or prospects to research databases such as those made available by the Securities and Exchange Commission (SEC) and the Financial Industry Regulatory Authority (finra.org).

Align yourself with an advisor who has been time-proven. Align yourself with an advisor who has been through multiple market cycles and periods of economic growth, as well as recessions. Align yourself with an advisor who has been to battle. These people are out there; it just takes a little research to find them!

The Ties That Bind

So what do salespeople, interior decorators, and the marketer extraordinaire have in common?

None of them are financial advisors with whom you want to do business!

Remember, a lot of people pose as financial advisors, and they will sell you everything—except for what you really need. Now you know how to spot these "posers," but there are other red flags to look out for as well.

Beware of the advisor who shows up at your door on a cold call. This is common with some brokerage firms that require their brokers to go door-to-door in the community to introduce themselves. Do you think advisors worth their salt would walk door-to-door? Or would they be busy handling their clients' affairs? Again, this practice is based on a sales-person mentality, as opposed to behaving like an advisor.

Another important consideration is whether to go with an independent advisor or a big chain. Which will serve you better? Although a chain might have name recognition and clout, independent advisors own their book of business. They have a vested interest in doing the right thing and building that business. People who work for a larger company are employees of that corporate entity. When they leave, new advisors are assigned to take over, regardless of whether or not they are a good fit for the clients. Independent advisors, on the other hand, look to build long-lasting relationships.

It's All about Communication

The foundation of a good relationship—whether it's with a significant other, a friend, or an advisor—is communication. In order to have a trusting bond, you must have an open line of communication and the ability to discuss whatever life may throw your way. Imagine if you couldn't discuss finances with your partner. Do you think the relationship could survive? The best-case scenario would be a strained relationship that might be salvaged with professional counseling.

It seems like an obvious—and avoidable—scenario, but, in fact, thousands of people enter into relationships where such a lack of communication is the norm. I'm talking, of course, about relationships with advisors who don't discuss their fees up front.

Most advisors base their salary on commissions, which is problematic, to say the least. Failing to disclose costs up front does not lend itself to transparency—and that's what we all want when we do business with someone. We want a transparent transaction with no hidden fees or surprise costs. This very lack of transparency is what has given Wall Street, the government, and banking such bad reputations. People sense that there are dealings going on behind closed doors, and it makes them feel uneasy. And I don't blame them.

A fee-based relationship, on the other hand—one in which all costs are noted and accounted for—aligns the interests of both parties. Clients know what they're paying for, as well as the value they should be receiving in exchange for that money. If advisors are not straightforward about what they're earning—and clients don't know what they're actually paying—how can clients determine whether they're getting value in exchange?

It all comes down to trust. Can you trust the person who is handling one of the most important aspects of your life? Can you talk face-to-face with him, ask questions, and get clear answers? If you've found someone who matches these criteria, then you're likely in good hands.

Remember, the best results come when clients align themselves with advisors who do what they say they're going to do, who will make prudent decisions. Such professionals talk to their clients not just when they're deciding whether to work together, but also throughout the relationship.

Quite frequently, a prospect enjoys the advisor up front. They get along great and the client becomes excited about the future. But soon, the advisor focuses on new clients, because that's how he makes money: by recruiting new customers. Before long, the client feels as if there's a lack of communication and the relationship withers and dies.

For the relationship with your advisor to work, you must be treated the same way day after day, year after year. It's about consistency. Align yourself with an advisor who has a consistent process. When you get together on the phone, expect a consistent agenda about what's to be done. When such a process is in place and you're treated the same way all the time by the entire office staff, and your needs are addressed in the same manner each time, you'll know your added value—and you'll know that the person you're working with is *truly* an advisor.

5

DCA: Dollar-Cost Averaging versus Drastic Course of Action

Have you ever made an emotional decision that turned out to be a wise one? Decision-making under pressure is a funny thing. When our emotions run high, we're more motivated to take action. That swell of adrenaline and anxiety makes the world seem as if it's going to end, and our emotions simply will not leave us alone until we *do* something. More often than not, what we do is a mistake.

This fight-or-flight reaction is programmed into our DNA as a survival mechanism. Although it was a lifesaver for our ancient ancestors fleeing from saber-toothed tigers, when it comes to financial decisions, this instinct often spells disaster.

Not all emotional decisions become matters of life or death, but even when we're faced with smaller decisions, our emotions can cloud our judgment. Think about it: If you're having a good day, you might feel extra generous when it comes to tipping your server at your favorite Italian restaurant. When your daughter asks for ten bucks to go to the movies, you might give her twenty. On the other hand, if you're feeling gloomy and stressed, you're probably more prone to snap at your kid when he tracks mud into the house. And what do you say afterward? "Sorry, I just had a bad day at work." That's because normally you wouldn't behave in such a way.

Emotions can make you behave in ways you typically wouldn't. Thank goodness, our loved ones tend to understand when we're having a bad day. But what about finances? They aren't so forgiving. When it comes to your money, emotions are your worst enemy.

DCA: The Good, the Bad, and the Ugly

Economics tends to reward rational decision making, but humans are emotional beings. Although we would like to think we always behave rationally, sometimes we don't. Consequently, swings in gas prices or the housing market spark emotional reactions, which often lead to bad decisions. And bad decisions prevent us from achieving our goals.

I like to think of it as the two schools of DCA. Traditionally, DCA stands for dollar-cost averaging, which is an investment technique that involves buying investments on a schedule that averages the total cost per share, lowering the overall cost from what it would be if the investments were purchased in one lump sum. While it does not guarantee investment success, dollar-cost averaging is a good, logical practice that can help you save money in the long run, and a good advisor will guide you in handling your finances with this in mind.

But DCA also stands for something very different: drastic course of action. As the name implies, a drastic course of action is dangerous because it's based on gut reactions and fear. You heard the neighbors are raking it in from a particular stock, so you just have to have it. Or an account lost value and now you want to sell all your shares? Beware! Taking a drastic course of action will sabotage your financial goals.

At the end of the day, you need a good plan, and you need to stick with it. And to have a good plan, you must keep emotions out of it.

Bad DCA: A National Pandemic

American economist Benjamin Graham once wisely wrote, "Bear markets are when stocks return to their rightful owners." A bear market signifies an economic shift. The perception during such a time is that investors should withdraw their money or stand to lose a great deal. As Graham suggests, this isn't necessarily the case. The emotional reaction that causes so many to get rid of their investments allows those who stand by logic to reap the benefits. In other words, those "rightful owners" are simply the investors who make good decisions during euphoric or drastic times.

So what's keeping you from making good decisions?

This impulsiveness is inherent in our society. When we see a 20-percent-off sale, we run out to buy what we perceive to be a sizzling deal. On Black Friday, we camp out in line or wake up at the crack of dawn to get first pick at the one-day-only holiday sales.

I'm sorry to burst your bubble if you're a Black Friday reveler, but studies have shown that the values are *the same* as during the time leading up to Christmas. Shoppers simply believe they're getting a better value on that day because of the advertising aimed at hyping up the sale, making them believe that this is a deal that won't last. My advice: Stay in bed! Hang out with your family. Don't let your emotions mislead you.

Another drastic course of action takes place when people listen to their coworkers or take tips from their neighbors about how they should handle their finances. To those tempted to follow the pack, I pose the following question: Would you take beauty tips from the butcher? (Hint: It's called a "butchered" haircut for a reason!) Ultimately, you need to work with professionals who have the specific knowledge required in their field.

Preparation: Making Your Own Luck

Listening to the noise of your friends and neighbors—and then acting on it—amounts to a random approach to what should be a deliberate financial strategy. This dilemma brings to mind a friend of mine who, at the end of coyote-hunting season each year, gathers a bunch of his buddies together for a bonfire. They sit around the fire and have drinks. Drinks lead to storytelling, and storytelling inevitably leads to the shooting of guns.

At first, they set the target six hundred yards away and take turns trying to hit it, but they never succeed. Eventually, they keep moving the target closer and closer, and at about two hundred yards, one of them will finally hit the target and revel in his excellent marksmanship. That's when they turn to my friend and taunt him for not taking a shot.

Why doesn't he take a shot? After all, he's been shooting guns longer than most of these guys have been alive. My friend doesn't take a shot, he says, because the key to success isn't talking a big game and taking random stabs at things; rather, it's preparation. Whenever he shoots at anything, he absolutely hates to miss; thus, when he shoots a gun, he knows he needs to rely on his extensive experience and ensure that his equipment is in proper working condition. He has to have a focused approach in order to succeed.

When I think of the smartest guy in the room, I think of my friend. Like my friend, the smartest guy in the room is the one who's focused on his goals, not the random shooter who doesn't prepare. The person who will reach his goals is the one who takes a calculated approach to hitting a target.

Walk the Walk— by Listening to the *Right Talk*

There are those who talk, and there are those who actually *do*. It's the people from the latter group that you want in your corner. The best way to insulate yourself from emotional decision making is to have someone in your corner who will be around to counsel you during those times when you need to make emotional decisions.

At our firm, during the last economic downturn, we called every one of our clients to offer a refresher course on bear markets and why they happen. We went over each client's plan and made sure every one of them understood how that plan would work. We wanted to ensure that our clients felt comfortable with the plans we had created for them.

If our clients ever have other ideas about what they'd like to do, we're always willing to listen. We offer them what we call "a cup of coffee and a second opinion." We're always willing to tell our clients honestly what we think of outside advice.

A Voice of Reason

I recently counseled a client who worked in the agricultural industry and came to me after a negative quarterly statement. His account value had gone down, and he wanted to know who had that money. He thought the market had taken it from him. I explained that in the grand scheme of his overall financial plan, this account was a small asset.

To help him understand, I asked, "Do farm values change?"

"Sure," he replied.

"And when they change, does someone lose money? If the value of your neighbor's farm changes, for example, do you lose money?"

Suddenly, he understood that statements and numbers are a snapshot in time, like turbulence on a flight, or a rainstorm in the summer. They're temporary and not indicative of the probable long-term outcome of any one plan. In the long run, we're all on a long-term trend toward stability. The problem is that most people don't have someone to explain this in terms they can understand, and so they're at the mercy of their emotions.

Money is just about the most emotional topic out there. When you throw in a layer of misunderstanding, it only fuels those emotions. The average person does not understand the technical considerations that affect a financial advisor's decisions. They don't understand P/E ratios and market caps. They don't understand share buybacks. There are many factors involved in mining for value that the average person simply doesn't know about. So when they look at the Standard & Poor's Index or the DOW, what they see is not an accurate representation of what's happening with their affairs.

If you don't understand the intricacies of the market, you may hear only what you want to hear, which, ultimately, is based on emotions and is far more negative. And that kind of negativity is not a good thing to have rattling around in your brain.

Advisors can't define outcomes, but they can use their extensive education and experience to assess a given situation and recommend what they feel is the best course of action. So give yourself a break and let an advisor you trust guide you.

6

Don't Expect an Online Advisor to Care about Your Kids

An accountant friend once told me a fascinating story about one of his clients, a hardworking Midwesterner who was planning for the future. Although I'm sure my friend shared the story for its bizarre details, it actually illustrates a practice I see again and again—and it needs to be stopped. I call it "The Cautionary Tale of the Golden Shrimp," and in telling you this story, I hope to spare you from a similar fate.

It all began with a phone call. One fateful evening, a man in Iowa, like millions of other frustrated and fed-up citizens across the country, received a call from the telemarketing abyss. But unlike most people, instead of sharing a few choice words and then hanging up, this man listened. He listened to what the telemarketer had to offer and waited silently on the phone as the telemarketer pitched his foolproof investment: a sprawling new shrimp-farm operation in Texas.

This was no ordinary shrimp farm. No, this was a *state-of-the-art* shrimp farm that would utilize cutting-edge technology to reduce costs and increase productivity. It was a shrimp farm to end all shrimp farms, a sure bet, something bound to make everyone involved lots of money (or so the telemarketer said). Those shrimp might as well be made of gold.

And from this one cold call, the hardworking Midwesterner was sold. So much for an IRA or mutual fund, this was going to be his big investment. He wrote out a check for thousands, uncorked his bottle of champagne, and waited for the money to roll in.

So where is he now?

Still waiting for those millions. Of course, there's a chance the shrimp farm could eventually succeed. And there's a chance the scratch-off ticket you pick up at the gas station could win you the jackpot—but would you risk your retirement on it? In the case of the shrimp farm, if the business really was a successful idea, do you think the company would be making cold calls to strangers in Iowa? No way! Why would they do that when Wall Street could simply write a check for the entire project?

And yet, if the pitch worked on this fellow from Iowa, who knows how many others put in their money as well. Why would anyone fall for it? Simple. We're so overwhelmed by the dream of *easy money* or an *easy fortune* that we'll believe just about anything. The idea of tremendous gains outweighs reason. And so we make mistakes.

We take multivitamins instead of just eating better food. As a result, we waste money and lose time because we're not treating our bodies right. We use coupons sent in the mail to buy products we don't even need. By taking advantage of "perceived deals," we actually lose more money than if we were to just buy what we need.

And here's the biggie: We use online financial-advisory services to handle our money. They pull us in with big promises and flashy software, but in the end, they only use us and abuse us. As a result, we lose out on money and even more important—our security.

The Internet Trap

With all the information in the world available at the click of a button, it's easy to believe that we can solve any problem that might come our way. If you can operate your cell phone or iPad, why shouldn't you be able to handle your financial future via an online platform—or what I like to call *robo-advisors*? These robo-advisors advertise low costs and make you feel as if you have more control through

45

mechanisms such as interactive online tools and around-the-clock support. But are their services really a better deal?

I compare the robo-advisor dilemma to automobile maintenance. You can wash your car and change your oil at home, all for a fraction of the price you would pay at a professional business. But are you really getting the best results? Layer in the value of your time—not to mention the other things you could be doing with it—and doing it yourself may actually amount to a net loss.

But our ideas about what constitutes *a deal* are often an illusion. We think that certain shortcuts will save us money and that certain expenses are a bad deal. We think that investing in a shrimp farm will guarantee our retirement and that the Internet can solve all of our problems, when we actually should run in the other direction—and fast.

The Opportunity Cost of a Relationship

When it comes to investing, it's important to remember what's called the *opportunity cost*—the loss of potential gain from other resources when one option is chosen.

For example, let's say you bought a bottle of wine for $50. After keeping it in your basement for twenty years, the bottle is now worth $200. If you drink that bottle of wine now, what does it actually cost you? Most people think the cost is $50, but really it's $200 because you could have sold it for that amount. The point is that if you're focused only on cost, you're never going to see the big picture.

There is another kind of "opportunity cost" when it comes to managing your finances, and that's the cost of the relationships you choose to keep—or not keep.

Everyone has the opportunity to be wealthy. A big part of that opportunity is the personal relationships you form. Some people choose to go it on their own in order to avoid the expense of working with an expert. The reality is that in the long run, a good advisor would save—and earn—far more money on their behalf than what they would have saved by not seeking financial services at all.

The other opportunity cost of not teaming with a good financial advisor is living with a whole lot of stress and anxiety. Having good counsel on your side will allow you to make decisions with confidence. The advisor will take the burden of making the best financial choices on your behalf off your shoulders. And that's what separates the wealthy from the rich and the poor: To be rich means you make a lot of money, but you spend a lot. To be poor means you spend everything—or more. To be wealthy means *you don't have to worry about anything.*

Let's say you buy five cars over the next five years. If you deal with the same business five times in a face-to-face manner, you will probably have a far better feeling about those deals than you would if you went out and bought each car from a different stranger off Craigslist.

It doesn't matter if it's a financial advisor or a car deal. It all goes back to the trust. If you have a robo-advisor, do you have someone on your side who will coach you through good times and not-so-good times, who will check in with you and make expert decisions on your behalf to help you reach your long-term goals?

Not really. As the name implies, you have a robot. And do you really want a robot controlling one of the most important aspects of your life? Unlike a human, a robot doesn't care about your kids going to college. Nor does that robot worry about whether your purchases support or sabotage your long-term goals.

So why use a robot at all?

To serve our clients, we reach out through email messages, phone calls, and meetings. We average eighty client touches per year. We aren't doing that as a sales tool. The purpose of our correspondence is to expand trust between us and to keep the lines of communication open so that clients will think of us when they're trying to make big decisions. That's the kind of service you just won't get with an online platform.

When it comes to investing, most high earners have financial advisors they communicate with regularly, even more frequently than they communicate with their accountants or lawyers. But guess what? You don't have to have millions of dollars to receive the same level of service. Everyone has the same issues with planning, cash flow, and taxes, and everyone can use someone on his team to guide him through those issues. We may not be able to beat a machine at chess, but when it comes to relationships and building wealth, the human does it better.

The Time/Money Paradox

Even as computers take on more of the heavy lifting in our everyday existence, we humans believe we have less and less time. And so we dream up more ways for the computer to do our work for us.

Need to buy your wife an anniversary gift? Order it online! Out of cat litter? Buy online! Double-bypass surgery? Do it online! OK, maybe that last one is a bit of an exaggeration, but you get the picture: The Internet has empowered us to be do-it-yourselfers. But there are some things that simply cannot be done on a computer. Take that double-bypass surgery, for instance. Unless you're truly crazy, you would never actually consider an online resource for surgery, but on a smaller scale, we make this mistake all the time.

For every itch, cough, or sneeze, many people's first line of defense is the all-powerful Google search engine. Rather than checking in with their doctor, they look up their symptoms online and take care of it on their own. As a result, they might see the doctor only if they're feeling very ill.

And how does that affect their treatment? Think about it: If you don't regularly check in with your doctor, does he know what to look for in terms of your overall health? How can he notice those small but significant changes if he doesn't see you regularly?

Or do you tend to see a different doctor each time you get sick? You could see three doctors and receive three separate diagnoses! One of them might interpret something that's normal for you as a serious health risk—or vice versa, and miss a big problem—simply because the only information he has is what he gathered that day.

On the flip side, by going in for yearly checkups, you build a close, trusting relationship with your doctor. Should anything abnormal occur, she has a better chance of detecting it simply because she knows you—your history, your family, where you work, what you eat—and she can prescribe a plan that complements your lifestyle.

Earlier in this book, I compared your financial advisor to your family doctor. Like your doctor, it's the advisor's job to tailor a plan that will maintain your financial health, helping you grow stronger in the long run. Now you can see why a robo-advisor simply can't compare to a real, live human being. If you wouldn't use an online doctor, why would you use an online advisor?

The Human Touch

Just because something is high-tech doesn't mean it's better for you. Just because something seems like a *better deal* doesn't mean it is. And for those times when you can't tell the difference, a trusted human can guide the way. On the road to achieving your dreams, the winning factor is the *human factor.*

Just as it is with your doctor, it's critical to develop a face-to-face dialogue with your advisor. Allow him the opportunity to learn about you, your goals, and all those other qualities that are unique to you, because that's the very information that will help him make the best decisions for you. That's the make-or-break element, the *special sauce,* when working with advisors: They understand you, as well as your past and future, and will help you achieve your goals. Anything less than that level of attention is a waste of your time. A robot may do a great job sweeping your floor, but when it comes to your money, get a human!

7

What Do You Do
with Eggs and a Basket?

Ah, the old adage, "Don't put all your eggs in one basket." Like most maxims, this one was invented to teach a valuable lesson: "Don't become dependent on one thing . . . because what happens when that one thing falls through?"

Though this might be sound wisdom for the racetrack or college admissions, for my area of expertise, it's a bunch of hogwash. There's a common mistake made in financial management, and it has everything to do with eggs and baskets: Instead of using one comprehensive advisor, people use multiple brokers and multiple banks—even if they own the exact same investments in each of those accounts.

They put their nest eggs in many different baskets, and they do this because they feel there's safety in having their assets spread around. If one basket fails, they have other eggs in other baskets to see them through. Or so the rationale goes.

What really happens is this: Rather than having safety, they have mismanagement. Rather than comprehensive growth, they have gaping holes in what should be greater returns. In exchange for using multiple brokers and advisors, they end up with a whole lot of confusion.

Using this old proverb as a guide really isn't the right way to look at managing your finances, because it's not about how many eggs you have in the basket; it's about how many people you have carrying the basket. If we are to apply this adage to your finances, it should read more like this: *Put your eggs in one basket. Just make sure you've got the right person carrying the basket.*

In the game of financial planning, it's important to team up with one advisor to carry your basket. Having a plan is far more important than protecting your pieces for a short journey, and having a plan means having one captain at the helm. By spreading your portfolio around, you fragment your finances. That may work for the short-term, but it takes into account only a slice of your overall assets and goals.

If your financial plan is spread across institutions, it means each one is managing a small piece of the puzzle, but nothing is actually fitting together. This division also gives you a false gauge of what equals success. If you have five different brokers and five different accounts, you'll zero in on the one who has the best results, and perhaps invest a little more with that one. Just because one of them has better results than the others doesn't mean you're headed in the right direction. In fact, you could be headed down a dangerous path.

One Plan, One Journey

If you have four kids, and you're going on a family vacation, are you going to take more than one vehicle? No way! You're taking the family van—and only after it's been oiled, safety-checked, and gassed up. On top of that, you'll make sure that van is filled with snacks, luggage, and entertainment for the road trip. Once you're on the road, you're following a precise route. Everything is mapped out to the smallest detail.

As you're driving across country, you don't pull up a navigation system and ask for ten different routes to get you where you want to go. Rather, you have one plan. You're navigating to one destination, not exploring every twist and turn in the road. Maybe you stop on the way, but you always have that destination in sight. To travel without a plan is to enter a void of insanity. You don't want five different journeys with five different navigators; you want one trip, one experience.

Having one long-term plan means that if there are bumps on the road or detours, you're still headed in the right direction to the ultimate destination. If you have someone on your side navigating the plan, that person will ensure you follow through until the very end.

One Road, Two-Way Conversation

I've touched on the values of having a trusted partner, one who can advise you during the most difficult times of your life and help you reach the most anticipated milestones. But how can you build trust with someone who has an interest in only one aspect of your life?

Consider it from the advisor's perspective: If your advisor knows he has only a small piece of your puzzle, how is that reflected in his performance? When you have money spread around in different places, it creates a snowball effect. The brokers don't have as deep a passion for your account, nor do they have a clear vision of what you want your future to look like. As a result, if you call them with requests during a wonderful stretch of market and everyone is buying Internet stocks, your broker might be less inclined to argue with you. They do as you ask, even though it will likely hurt you in the long run.

Or perhaps that broker will recommend allocations that aren't appropriate because he or she is trying to garner business. Having multiple brokers leads to a transaction-based mentality. The process becomes a one-way chain of command instead of a two-way conversation. If you're all-in with one planner, however, you're on track for a long-term journey. Your work is not about one-time transactions over the phone, but rather, the larger plan.

Before You Have a Basket, You Must Have an Egg

What's the use of discussing who should carry your basket if you don't have any eggs stored away in the first place? Young people think they can't afford to save. To all of you out there who might relate to that situation, I say this: There is no amount too small to put away. You never run into someone who says, "Gosh, I wish I didn't save so much!" Most people regret things that they didn't do, not the things they did.

But the problem remains: For millions of people, it is incredibly difficult to get started with savings. The number-one thing that prevents them from growing their own nest egg is confusion about their finances. Even those who don't realize they're confused are often confused.

The solution is simple: Get help. Find someone who knows what you don't know. After all, that's what the wealthiest people in our nation do, and it's a formula you can emulate. As I mentioned in the previous chapter, wealthy individuals are far more likely to have a close relationship with a financial advisor than with a lawyer, accountant, or doctor. A friend of mine who works on the floor of the New York Stock Exchange once said, "Money isn't everything, but it's right behind oxygen."

No matter who you are, if you think money isn't important, think again. It is. But it's not about how much you have; it's about what you do with what you have. It's becoming ingrained in our society that we can't live without pricey goods and services. We have to have iPhones and unlimited data plans and all of the companion technology that comes along with it. That means that for the rest of your life, you're spending $100 a month on things that, in theory, don't necessarily improve your life. In fact, if you've seen all the recent reports on the effects of social media and smartphones on happiness and intelligence, you just might toss that iPhone out the window.

People are addicted to things that cost money when they should be addicted to things that save money. Why is it OK to give Verizon $100 a month when you won't even pay yourself? What if with every text we sent, a penny went into our savings account? That would be a life-changing event! Believe it or not, those pennies add up (especially when some people average hundreds of texts per day!).

The biggest problem with smart phones is that they increase our need for instant gratification. As a result, we live in the present or in the next second. A "New York minute" has become something more like a "Facebook second." What we need more than anything is a long-term plan.

No advisor or entity can help you unless you have the desire to help yourself. With that small shift in attitude, you can do great things with what you have. If you're one of those people who have not yet started saving, you need assistance more than anyone else. A good advisor or planner in your corner will not chide or embarrass you, but he will push you down the right path.

Keeping the Eggs Safe in the Nest

At the end of the day, people use multiple advisors because the old adage makes it seem like the right thing to do. And so it breeds false comfort.

But if you find the right advisor, he will make a plan and make decisions according to that plan. In the end, you'll be more comfortable than you would ever have imagined. Regardless of your age, what you're putting in place with an advisor is a long-term plan, whether it's for you, your kids, your spouse, a charity, or any other entity.

An investment plan for the next five years is not a plan. That's a brief window of time. That's leaving money in the bank. A financial plan is from now until death. As long as you're on this earth, and even after, your plan continues the way you want it to play out. Any strategy with a specific ending date is just a segment within the plan. And so a good planner or advisor will help you navigate each portion of the journey to completion while keeping the big picture in mind.

Having a good advisor does not mean all the money is under the management of that advisor. In fact, if the next step in your plan is to put money in a bank, then that's what the advisor will tell you to do. He will aim for the most favorable outcome. By using multiple advisors, you remain focused on the segments.

If you want to enjoy your full life journey, you want your eggs in one basket. Because those eggs are going to pay for everything you want in life—charity donations, a second home, sending your kids to college. Just make sure you find the right person to help you carry that basket.

8

Don't Be Normal, Be Boring

According to an Employee Benefit Research Institute and Greenwald & Associates survey,[1] nearly a third of workers have less than $1,000 in savings that could be applied toward their retirement. When you consider that cold, hard fact, one question comes to mind: What happened to their money?

The same thing that happened to everyone else's money: They spent it.

People spend money for more reasons than there are drops of water in the ocean. Sometimes the amount of

---

1 https://www.ebri.org/pdf/surveys/rcs/2015/RCS15.FS-3.Preps.pdf

money we spend is out of our control; we get sick, we have emergencies, and we have huge necessary expenses. Other times, however, our spending is completely within our control. We spend—and spend big—on new technology, new clothes, new cars, new homes, and much, much more. Be it out of necessity or desire, our spending determines whether or not we reach our retirement goals, and our spending is determined by our personalities.

Spenders versus Savers

At the end of the day, humans are hardwired to be either spenders or savers. And unlike most human characteristics, there is very little gray zone in between. Nor is there an even division of spenders and savers. In fact, the scales tip heavily on the side of the all-mighty-dollar spender.

Our society is built on consumerism; it thrives on the spenders. Purchasing goods is praised as sound economics, and, indeed, commerce is necessary to keep our country alive and functioning. This proliferation of spenders may be beneficial to corporations, but it's also responsible for a harrowing financial statistic, the one that shows people are spending far too much, leaving many of them unable to maintain their lifestyles after retirement.

What can we do to change it? The answer is education. By now, you've gained a lot of knowledge about how to handle your money. We've talked about money myths and finding the right person to plan your future. But one thing we haven't covered is spending.

In the world of financial planning, talking about future goals is the easy part. It's not difficult to imagine what you want your life to look like ten, fifteen, or even fifty years down the line. This is especially true as you enter what I call the One Zone, that critical time when you're nearing retirement and it's time to make a definitive plan.

Spending, however, is a different subject. In a world dominated by spenders, who wants to talk about saving? Well, we're not going to talk about saving. We're going to talk about spending—that is, spending the *right way*.

Keep Your Financial Life Boring

Boring is good. In fact, boring is beautiful. In finance, being boring means you don't think like the herd. You don't accept the one-size-fits-all mentality, and you don't buy into the norm. Right now, that norm is Black Friday. The norm is purchasing on credit items that would otherwise be out of reach—and then defaulting. The norm is buying stuff instead of buying a future. The normal mentality is a spending mentality. It's the *I need this and I can't live without it* mentality. That's the fib we tell ourselves, that we can't live without it. But at the end of the day, these items aren't necessities; they're wants. And people have many more wants than needs.

If the constant barrage of advertising at every turn doesn't prove that we live in a culture where consuming is out of control, then consider all the shows on television these days about people who can't curb their wants (for example, *Hoarders*). These hoarders—people who can't stop accumulating *stuff*—are becoming the norm. Can you imagine if someone made a TV show about money hoarders? No one would even tune in! It would be boring.

And that's why boring is good. When we're talking about your financial future, boring is beautiful. But normal? That's not so nice.

In building wealth, we want your pathway to be so solid and sound that the thought of it could put you to sleep. We want the financial side of retirement to be boring so the day-to-day side of life can be active and enjoyable. By making your financial life a little more boring, you can relax into your everyday experience knowing that your future will be brighter.

Seeding Your Future by Spending the Right Way

The Scottish poet Alexander Smith wrote, "A man does not plant a tree for himself. He plants it for posterity." So here's the question: What's more important to you: your family and future generations or *the stuff*?

If you follow the norm and focus on spending to buy stuff throughout your life, you probably won't have much money left to pass on to the next generation. But if you change your mentality and embrace the power of planning and managing your finances, you can build a legacy and achieve all your goals. And the best way to begin building your legacy is to understand the effect spending has on your future.

Instead of spending on stuff, spend your money on your future—through smart investments. It's a simple concept, and yet so many people fail to embrace it. Many people believe investments are risky business. They think, *Why would I spend my money on the stock market when I could use it on something for which the value is guaranteed? Besides, the stock market is volatile—isn't it?*

Well, is it?

Think about airplanes. More precisely, think about flying. Flight has come a long way since the Wright brothers' first takeoff and landing. Today, it's even safer to fly from one state to another than it is to drive down the road to the grocery store. If you think about all the flights that get safely to their destinations day after day, year after year, the total number of disasters is really quite small. In other words, the risk factor of flight is close to zero.

The real trouble with flying is in everything else surrounding the actual flight: waiting in line, flight delays, being forced to buy bad food that costs a fortune, and more. But at the end of the day, we put up with these inconveniences. We endure TSA pat-downs and overcrowded gates. More important, we accept the minimal risk involved with flying—the potential volatility inherent in the remote possibility of a disaster—because it's worth it.

What about the risks that come with investing?

While all investing involves some degree of risk, if your time horizon is long enough—say, over fifteen years—the chance of losing money on a well-constructed, well diversified portfolio approaches zero. The real risk is not being educated and *not* investing.

Throughout the history of the stock market, there have been highs and lows. Even in really good years, there's always volatility, regardless of political events. Volatility is normal. Without volatility, the stock market would be boring. Prices would stair-step up. With volatility, you can buy stocks on sale, so to speak. And since we have volatility, it makes sense to invest each month without overthinking it—as we discussed in Chapter 6, in our discussion of dollar-cost averaging. As a result, you're buying low and selling high in the long run.

Volatility is a temporary hiccup. It's turbulence on the flight. It's normal, and in the end, you're still going to arrive at the same destination. So start spending your money today on your future—and invest!

Embrace Optimism

Even if you know investing your money in the stock market is the smart thing to do, sometimes it's difficult to feel at ease with your decision because of all the doom and gloom that appears in the news these days. We live in a pessimistic world, but when did pessimism ever help anything? We need a good dose of optimism if we want to succeed.

At the end of the day, people are smart. They solve problems. So you can't focus on headlines about the country hitting its debt ceiling, because in the long run, it won't matter. Regardless of a person's age, everyone thinks about how much the world has changed around him in his lifetime. Every person of every generation has wondered how the world wound up in such chaos.

What does that tell you? It tells you the world is *not* chaotic! The world simply changes, and ultimately, it's changing for the better. The world is optimistic. So get with the program.

The downside to being a pessimistic spender is that you'll never be successful, because you'll never be truly happy or satisfied. Pessimism, by definition, is the tendency to see the worst in things, to stick to the negatives and never be forward-thinking. Negative people will never be happy.

But there's no reason to be negative. The facts are these: Economies gain in size, the population grows, and there's more demand for goods and services. Technology improves. And so spending your money on the market will reward you.

The New School of Smart Spending

Be deliberate with what you spend, because when you're wise with your money, spending it is actually investing it. Spend on your future, not on an iPhone. Spend on your legacy, not on a designer suit. Spend on a plan, not on a temporary distraction. If you don't have the knowledge to execute a plan yourself, spend on services that will get it done for you.

Every tangible thing you buy in life is sold to you. Arguably, the only time you get your money's actual value is when you purchase a service. You get what you pay for, whether it's an accountant, a lawyer, or a financial advisor. Advisors are looking ahead to a point in the future and determining how to get there in the best possible fashion. They will help you see past the noise and pessimism, and help tame your deep-seated impulses. Partner with an advisor who has the drive to succeed and the ability to show you that being boring can actually be downright amazing.

9

Don't Stop Here

When I meet new people, whether at a social function, while traveling, or at a friend's backyard barbecue, inevitably this question gets asked: "What do you do for a living?"

"I'm a financial planner," I respond—loud and proud—and then I wait for them to flinch. You see, when I tell people that I offer financial-planning services, they always hesitate. It's as if they're afraid I'm going to try to sell them something. And I understand that reaction. So many businesspeople are all about the hustle, the ten-second elevator pitch they keep on hand for every new face they meet. Every stranger, friend, and relative is a prospect.

And I think that approach to business prospects is just ridiculous.

I don't believe in the elevator pitch. Nor do I believe in talking shop while there's ketchup running down my shirt. My motto is this: Do a good job, enjoy what you do, and people will come to you. It's as simple as that.

I feel incredibly privileged to have experienced such harmony. I love what I do; I work hard; and in return, I've been able to assist thousands of people with one of the most important aspects of their lives. And through this experience, I've also learned that those thousands are but a fraction of the people who need assistance. Maybe it's the stigma associated with financial planners or businesspeople in general, but far too many people are going without the kind of help that would greatly enhance their lives.

I believe that most people want assistance so that they can improve themselves. Most people are open-minded about receiving advice and working with an advisor, but they feel a certain discomfort about taking the first step. They wonder, *How do I know this person will help me? How do I even know what I need?*

Now that you've made it this far into the book, you have the answers to those questions. You know how to identify who can help you, and you understand what you need. Let's recap here the other things you've learned about how to stop doing dumb things with your money.

Don't buy more financial services than you need. With such a large number of products and add-ons available, you could easily end up spending far more than you would actually save with these so-called financial-planning tools. There is such a thing as going overboard, just as there are offerings that don't really do much for your money. You're entitled to certain value offerings as a client. Find an advisor who can deliver on those values and provide the service you deserve.

Don't set insane goals. Goals are good, as long as they're within the realm of possibility. The get-rich-quick mentality pervades common thinking when it comes to investing and making money. There is a tried-and-true method of building wealth, but it takes time, consistency, and effort. Oh, and did I mention time? Your most important financial goals are on a long-term time horizon, so settle in for the journey.

Don't confuse long-term goals with accumulating money in the bank. In fact, leaving money in the bank can actually cost you money in the end. Invest, but invest wisely with your own unique plan in mind.

Don't hire an advisor who's not an advisor. In an industry that has more than its share of masqueraders, how can you spot the true financial advisors? Be on the lookout for the three kinds of imitators: There are the salespeople, who talk at you more than they listen to your needs. There are the interior decorators, who are more concerned with appearances than the value of their services. And then there are the marketing experts, who are top-notch at selling themselves but not necessarily skilled at meeting your goals.

What's the best way to determine whether your advisor checks out? Talk to him. A good financial advisor will be able to answer all your questions and will take the time to make sure your needs are met and that you're on track with a solid long-term plan.

Don't take a drastic course of action. It's easy to be swayed by your friends' and neighbors' emotions. When you hear rave reviews about the latest blockbuster, what do you want to do? Go see the movie, of course! And if everyone says it stinks? You bypass the box office and Netflix it.

Don't make the same mistake with your investments. Unlike going to see a bad movie, the mistake is not merely the cost of admission; it is the price of retirement. Stick to sound reason, and stick to the facts. Dollar-cost averaging will allow you to grow your wealth with the greatest amount of security. To do that, you have to shut out the noise.

Don't expect an online advisor to care about your kids. A robot does not have feelings; a robot does not love; a robot does not care if your kids go to college or if you can afford to keep your house after retirement. Why allow an Internet robot to control one of the most important aspects of your life when it doesn't care about the things that are most important to you? In the battle of man versus robot, humans do it better. Stick with a warm-blooded person to keep your finances in line and your kids in college.

Keep your eggs in one basket; just make sure you have the right person carrying it. Throw the old wisdom out the window. Security does not come from spreading your assets among banks and brokers. Security comes from having one comprehensive plan, and one entity making sure every factor of your portfolio is supporting that plan.

Store up your nest eggs, and find the best person to carry the basket for you.

Don't do what's normal; do what's boring. It's OK if the thought of budgeting and investing and diversifying doesn't excite you. But for goodness' sake, don't follow the norm and let consumerism consume you! Herd mentality is why more than two-thirds of adults retire with less than $25,000 to their names. So cut ties with the norm and find a trustworthy advisor to handle the boring task of keeping your money safe—which, in the end, is actually pretty exciting!

Act on What You've Learned

As we've discussed, growing wealth and maintaining security comes down to education. Those who are educated in finance will make well-informed decisions with their money. But most of us simply don't have that education because it's not readily available. There was no course called Introduction to Managing Money when I was in high school.

Although not all of us have access to a financial education, every single person has access to an expert. And the sooner you link up with a person who can help you, the stronger your portfolio will grow. So go out and take action. Go out and find someone to help you stop doing dumb things with your money. Do it sooner rather than later, because one day there will come a boiling point.

Entering the One Zone

Early in life, there are a lot of variables that determine what will become of us. In our twenties, we're still figuring out our careers, dreaming about where we'll live, and maybe even how many kids we'll have. It's difficult to know definitively what we'll need later in life.

As you near retirement, you reach what I call the One Zone. The One Zone means that no matter what's happened up to this point, this is your one chance to get retirement right. This is the time to consolidate your advisors, to bring the plan together. Otherwise, you'll have chaos, and that chaos can't be overcome. To prevent yourself from going down that road, team up with someone who has been there before and who can help you down the path.

Anybody can think, reason, and plan as well as the sharpest people in the world. Your ability to plan for the future doesn't come down to your own talents; it comes down to your ability to align yourself with the right people.

A good advisor can team up with you no matter where you are on your life's journey. If you're a young person, that advisor can explain the importance of budgeting, saving, and getting the right interest rate on your mortgage. If you're older, on the other hand, an advisor will help ensure you have everything on track for a healthy retirement.

As you go from career to career, that advisor can assist you in doing the right thing with your retirement plan and life insurance. A good advisor can ask you the right questions. So if you want to escape being normal, somewhere along the journey you need to reach out and work with an advisor—or you risk being normal and having to work the rest of your days. What choice will you make?

It's Time to Say Hello

I wrote this book to open people's minds to the possibility that there might be someone out there who can help them, no matter where they are or where they want to go. I saw what the stereotypes and misconceptions about financial advisors were doing to people who otherwise could have avoided financial strife. I wrote this book to inform people that there are advisors out there who aren't trying to sell something. There are advisors out there whose passion is to help their clients live the lives they want. Wherever you live, I want you to find an advisor like that. And if you can't find one, call me and I will point you in the right direction.

So stop doing dumb things with your money, and make the smartest decision: Go out and take action. Start working toward the financial picture of your dreams. It's possible. All it takes is the right partnership to form the perfect plan.